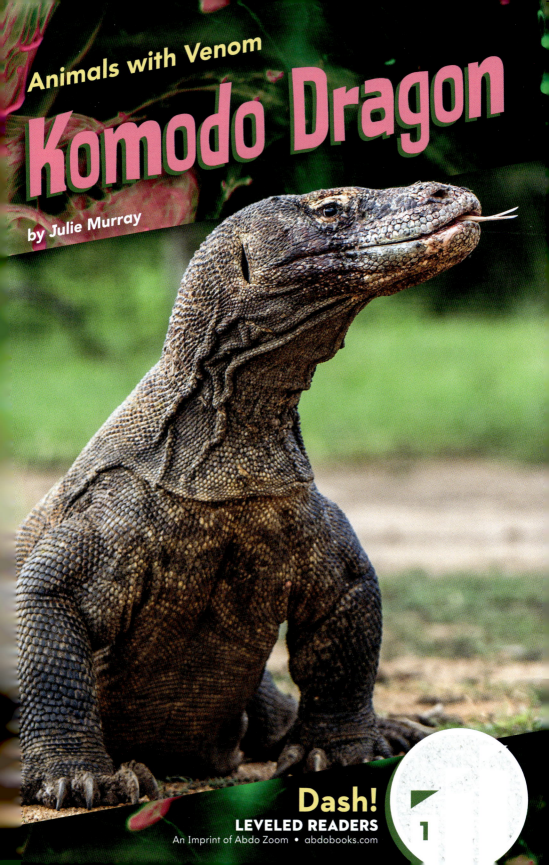

Animals with Venom
Komodo Dragon

by Julie Murray

Dash!
LEVELED READERS
1
An Imprint of Abdo Zoom • abdobooks.com

Dash!
LEVELED READERS

Level 1 – Beginning
Short and simple sentences with familiar words or patterns for children who are beginning to understand how letters and sounds go together.

Level 2 – Emerging
Longer words and sentences with more complex language patterns for readers who are practicing common words and letter sounds.

Level 3 – Transitional
More developed language and vocabulary for readers who are becoming more independent.

abdobooks.com

THIS BOOK CONTAINS RECYCLED MATERIALS

Published by Abdo Zoom, a division of ABDO, PO Box 398166, Minneapolis, Minnesota 55439. Copyright © 2021 by Abdo Consulting Group, Inc. International copyrights reserved in all countries. No part of this book may be reproduced in any form without written permission from the publisher. Dash!™ is a trademark and logo of Abdo Zoom.

Printed in the United States of America, North Mankato, Minnesota.
052020
092020

Photo Credits: Alamy, iStock, Shutterstock
Production Contributors: Kenny Abdo, Jennie Forsberg, Grace Hansen, John Hansen
Design Contributors: Dorothy Toth, Neil Klinepier, Candice Keimig

Library of Congress Control Number: 2019956167

Publisher's Cataloging in Publication Data

Names: Murray, Julie, author.
Title: Komodo dragon / by Julie Murray
Description: Minneapolis, Minnesota : Abdo Zoom, 2021 | Series: Animals with venom | Includes online resources and index.
Identifiers: ISBN 9781098221041 (lib. bdg.) | ISBN 9781644943991 (pbk.) | ISBN 9781098222024 (ebook) | ISBN 9781098222512 (Read-to-Me ebook)
Subjects: LCSH: Komodo dragon--Juvenile literature. | Dragon lizards--Juvenile literature. | Monitor lizards--Juvenile literature. | Poisonous animals--Juvenile literature. | Bites and stings--Juvenile literature.
Classification: DDC 591.69--dc23

Table of Contents

Komodo Dragon 4

More Facts 22

Glossary 23

Index 24

Online Resources 24

Komodo Dragon

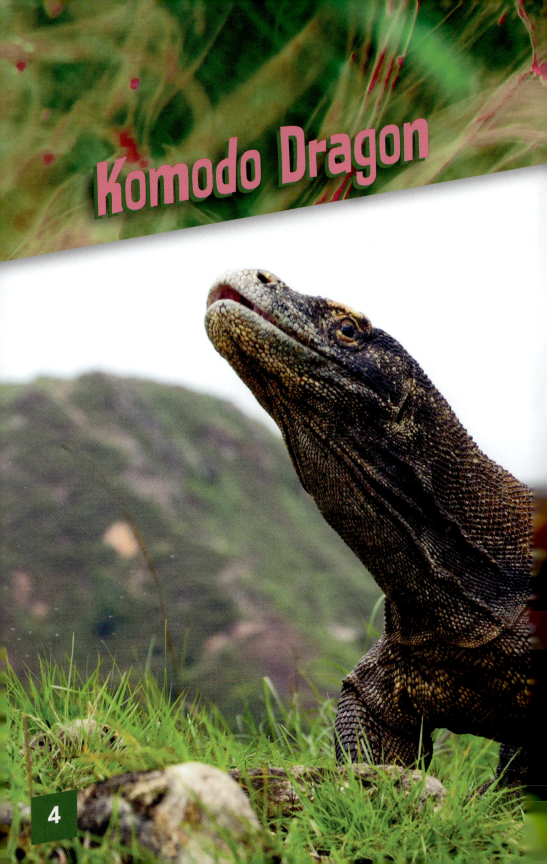

Komodo dragons live on small islands in **Indonesia**. It is dry and hot there.

A Komodo dragon is a **reptile**. It is cold-blooded and has scales. It warms itself in the sun.

A **burrow** keeps the Komodo dragon cool during the day and warm at night.

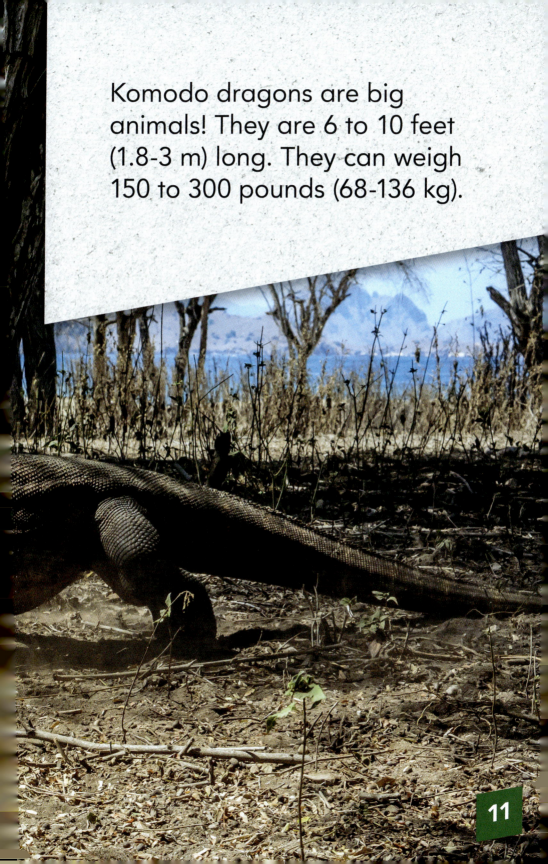

Komodo dragons are big animals! They are 6 to 10 feet (1.8-3 m) long. They can weigh 150 to 300 pounds (68-136 kg).

Komodo dragons have thick bodies. They can be brown, gray, or dull red in color.

They have short, strong legs. They have a long tail. Their claws are sharp.

A Komodo dragon has a **forked** tongue. It uses its tongue to smell **prey** up to 7 miles (11.3 km) away!

17

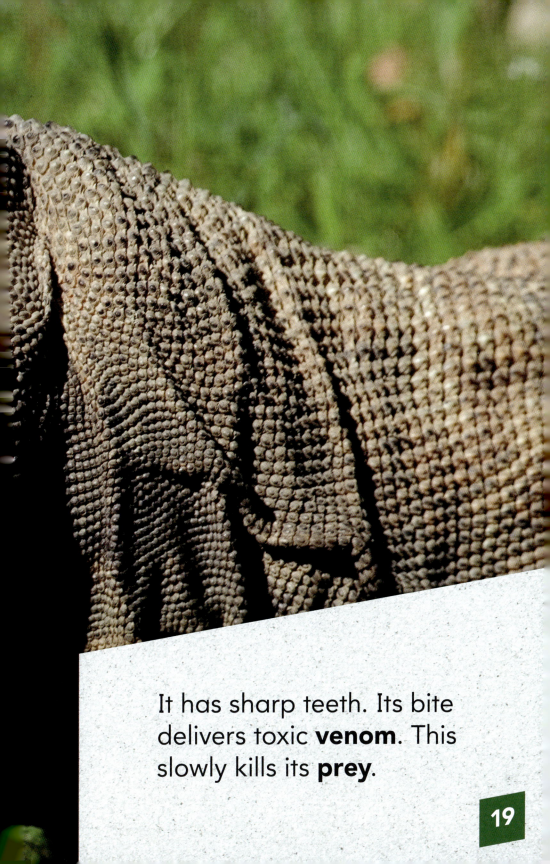

It has sharp teeth. Its bite delivers toxic **venom**. This slowly kills its **prey**.

Komodo dragons eat meat. They eat deer, goats, water buffalo, and more.

More Facts

- Komodo dragons can run 10 mph (16 km/h) for short distances.

- They can live up to 50 years in the wild.

- About 6,000 of these big **reptiles** live in Komodo National Park in **Indonesia**.

Glossary

burrow – a hole or tunnel dug by certain animals for use as a hiding place or home.

forked – having a divided or pronged end.

Indonesia – a country in southeastern Asia made up of islands stretching from the Indian Ocean into the Pacific Ocean. Jakarta is the capital of Indonesia.

prey – an animal that is hunted and eaten by another animal.

reptile – a cold-blooded animal with a skeleton inside its body and dry scales or hard plates on its skin.

venom – a poison that certain animals make.

Index

body 12
burrow 9
claws 15
climate 5
color 12
food 16, 19, 20
habitat 5
Indonesia 5
legs 15
scales 6
size 11
teeth 19
tongue 16
venom 19

Online Resources

To learn more about Komodo dragons, please visit abdobooklinks.com or scan this QR code. These links are routinely monitored and updated to provide the most current information available.